The Curious Tiger

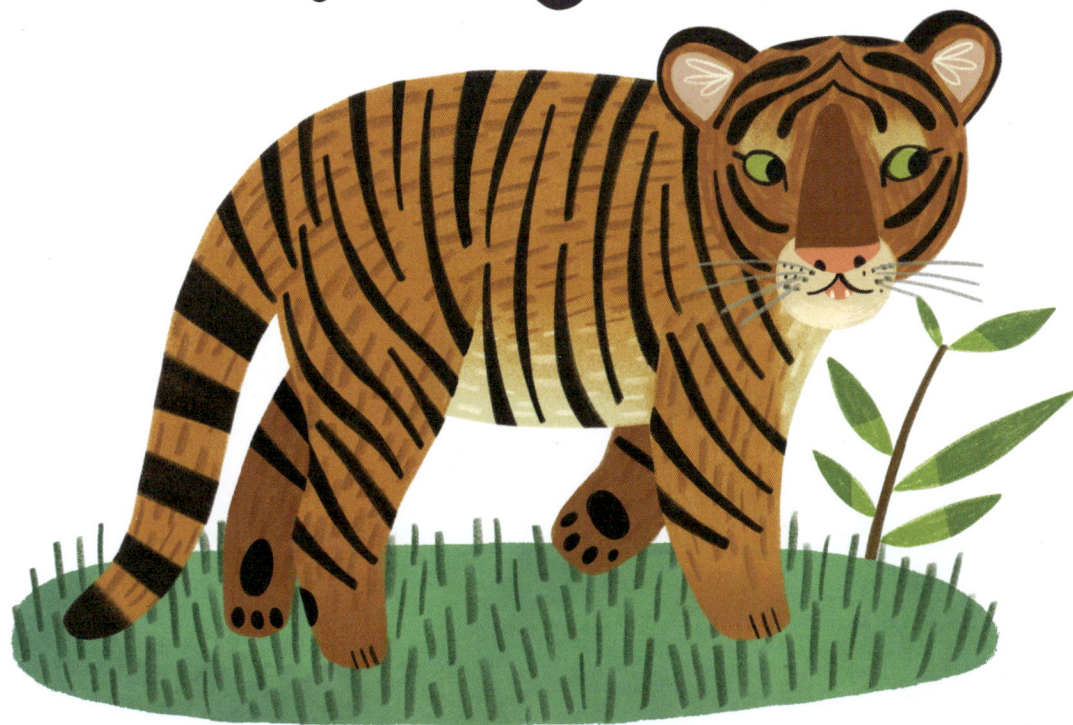

Written by Catherine Veitch   Illustrated by Jean Claude

MILES KELLY

One evening, a mother tiger was taking her cubs, Tejas and Tara, through the forest. She wanted to teach them which animals to hunt for food. Tejas was always asking questions. But his mother did not mind, because being curious helped Tejas learn.

"Will we catch any animals?" he asked.

"Not this evening because our tummies are full," said his mother.

Silently they crept through the mangrove forest and soon they spotted an animal snuffling in the wet mud.

"That's a wild boar," whispered mother tiger. "Wild boars are very tasty!"

Mother tiger and Tara carried on, but Tejas stayed behind. "Excuse me," he said to the boar, who was called Bristi, "what do you eat?"

Bristi looked fearfully at the tiger cub,
but could see that his tummy was full.

I like eating roots and shoots.

"Where were you?" scolded Tara,
as Tejas caught up with his family.

"Sssh!" said their mother. She was watching
a monkey up in the trees. Tejas' mother told
him it was a macaque, which is delicious.

Once again Tejas stayed behind. He asked the macaque, who was called Mitu, "What are you eating?"

"I'm snacking on some fruit before bedtime," replied Mitu. She felt perfectly safe high up in her tree.

"Try to keep up!" said Tara, as Tejas joined his family again.

"Quiet now!" said mother tiger. "Can you see a spotted deer? Tigers love eating deer."

Tejas was bursting with questions to ask the deer, so he hung back. The deer could tell that Tejas was not hungry. He said his name was Divum and that he liked to nibble leaves.

Tejas had learnt so much from asking questions.

"I have something else to show you," said mother tiger.

She took the cubs to a part of the forest
where there were no longer any trees.
Tejas could not believe what he saw.

What's happened to the trees?

"They have been chopped down," replied his mother.

"But why?" asked Tejas.

"To make room for other things," said his mother.

Mother tiger continued, "Because there is no forest here anymore, there are no wild boars, no macaques and no spotted deer, as there is no food or shelter for them."

"We can't stay here either, can we?" said Tejas. "There are no animals for us to eat."

It was time to head back into the forest.

Tejas needed cheering up, so mother
tiger took the cubs swimming.
All tigers love swimming!

"Race you to the river," shouted Tara,
who was almost there already.

SPLASH!

In the river Tejas met an otter. He could not stop himself asking another question.

"What do you like to eat?"

"I especially like eating crabs," replied Oditi the otter, who was a much better swimmer than any tiger.

"If otters eat crabs,
what do crabs eat?"
Tejas asked his mother.

"Why don't you ask one?" replied
mother tiger. So Tejas swam over to the soggy,
muddy bank to find some crabs.

The crabs sank back into the mud when they saw Tejas. But Choti, a brave fiddler crab, nipped Tejas' paw and said,

I nibble on dead animals, which keeps the river clean.

There were so many animals living in the mangrove forest and word quickly spread that a curious tiger cub was asking questions.

Animals grew bold and came out of their hiding places. A crocodile snapped that it liked to eat snakes, a snake hissed that it ate birds, and a bird quacked that it snacked on crabs.

Hiss hiss!

Soon it was time for the tigers to head back to their favourite spot under a mangrove tree to sleep.

Tejas did a big tigery shake to dry off. He was bubbling with excitement all the way home and could not stop chatting, telling Tara everything he had learnt that evening.

Tejas didn't want a story for bedtime.
He wanted to hear more about his forest.

"By asking questions I found out that some animals eat plants. And that others, like us tigers, eat animals," he told his mother. "Is there anything that hunts tigers?"

"I'll answer that question when you're a little older," said mother tiger. "But learning all about the forest will help to keep you safe. Goodnight, Tejas."

ZZZZZ

The
End